Eleanor Roosevelt

A Photo-Illustrated Biography
by Lucile Davis

Content Consultant:
Elizabeth Bethel Maset
Eleanor Roosevelt Researcher
Instructor of Government
Dutchess Community College

Bridgestone Books

an imprint of Capstone Press

Facts about Eleanor Roosevelt

- Eleanor Roosevelt was a niece of President Theodore Roosevelt.
- She was the First Lady of the United States for 12 years.
- She received more than 30,000 letters a month when she was First Lady.
- She was a member of the first U.S. delegation to the United Nations.

Bridgestone Books are published by Capstone Press
818 North Willow Street, Mankato, Minnesota 56001 • http://www. capstone-press.com
Copyright © 1998 by Capstone Press • All rights reserved • Printed in the United States of America

Library of Congress Cataloging-in-Publication Data
Davis, Lucile.
   Eleanor Roosevelt: a photo-illustrated biography/by Lucile Davis.
   p. cm.
   Includes bibliographical references and index.
   Summary: Presents the life story of the First Lady who worked for human rights and became known as the First Lady of the World.
   ISBN 1-56065-572-0
   1. Roosevelt, Eleanor, 1884-1962--Pictorial works--Juvenile literature. 2. Presidents' spouses--United States--Biography--Pictorial works--Juvenile literature. [1. Roosevelt, Eleanor, 1884-1962. 2. First ladies. 3. Women--Biography.] I. Title.
E807.1.R48D39   1998
973.917'092--dc21
                           97-5173
                           CIP
                           AC

Photo credits
Archive Photos, cover, 6, 10
UPI/Corbis-Bettman, 4, 8, 12, 14, 16, 18, 20

Table of Contents

Famous Leader

Eleanor Roosevelt worked her entire life to help people. She did all she could for the poor and others in need. She taught school, gave speeches, and led volunteers. Volunteers are people who work to help others without being paid.

Eleanor was married to Franklin Delano Roosevelt. He was president of the United States for 12 years. Eleanor was the First Lady. The First Lady is the wife of the president. Eleanor traveled and gave speeches as the First Lady. She listened to people's problems. People felt she was their friend.

Eleanor was also a famous worker for human rights. Human rights are the rights of all people to be treated fairly.

Eleanor became a member of the first U.S. delegation to the United Nations. A delegation is a group that speaks for a country. The United Nations is a group of countries that works for peace.

Eleanor became a member of the first U.S. delegation to the United Nations.

A Shy Child

Eleanor Roosevelt was born on October 11, 1884, in New York City. Her parents were Anna and Elliott. They named her Anna Eleanor. But people always called her Eleanor.

Eleanor was shy and quiet as a young girl. She was not pretty. Her mother worried about Eleanor's plain looks. Eleanor's father was not worried. He thought Eleanor was wonderful. She and her father enjoyed many happy times together.

Eleanor's father gave his time and money to help people. He wanted Eleanor to help, too. One day, he took Eleanor to a Thanksgiving party for homeless boys. Eleanor and her father helped give the boys food. Helping the boys made Eleanor feel useful.

Eleanor was eight years old when her mother died. Two years later, her father died. Eleanor went to live with her grandmother.

Eleanor (on right) was shy and quiet as a young girl.

Going to School

In 1899, Eleanor went to England. She was 15 years old. She went to a school for girls called Allenswood.

Marie Souvestre was in charge of the school. She became Eleanor's teacher and friend. Miss Souvestre gave Eleanor confidence. Confidence is a strong belief in yourself. Eleanor was a good student. Her new confidence helped her become a leader at school.

Eleanor went back to New York when she was 18. She began teaching at a school for poor people. She still liked helping others.

Eleanor had a distant cousin named Franklin Delano Roosevelt. Eleanor and Franklin saw each other at parties. They began dating. One day, Franklin asked Eleanor to marry him.

Eleanor and Franklin were married in 1905. Eleanor's uncle was President Theodore Roosevelt. He was president from 1901 to 1909. He walked Eleanor down the aisle at her wedding.

Eleanor married Franklin Roosevelt in 1905.

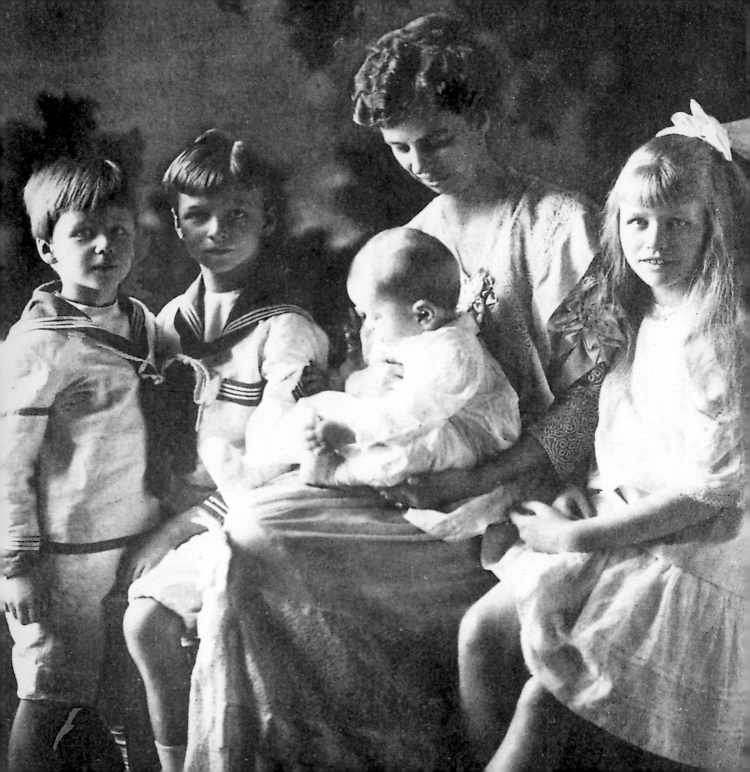

Wife, Mother, and Volunteer

Eleanor and Franklin settled in New York in 1905. Their first child was born the next year. They named her Anna. Eleanor and Franklin had four more children. Their names were James, Elliott, Franklin Jr., and John. Eleanor had one baby who died.

Franklin began his career in politics in 1910. He ran for New York state senator and won. Eleanor helped Franklin with his career. She learned about politics. She planned meetings and parties.

Franklin was given a leadership position in the U.S. Navy in 1913. The Roosevelt family moved to Washington, D.C. Eleanor led Red Cross workers there. The Red Cross is a worldwide group. It helps people who are hurt by floods, wars, and other troubles. Eleanor helped soldiers during World War I (1914-1918).

Eleanor and Franklin had a family after moving to New York.

Helping Her Husband

Franklin became very sick in the summer of 1921. He had a high fever. His legs became stiff. He could not move them.

The doctors said Franklin had polio. Polio is a disease that attacks the brain and spine. The doctors told Eleanor that Franklin would never walk again. Franklin's mother wanted him to stop working. But Eleanor knew Franklin would not be happy without work to do. He wanted to return to politics.

Eleanor wanted to help her husband. She learned that she could take her husband's place. Eleanor began going places Franklin could not go. She went to political meetings in his place.

Eleanor was asked to make speeches. Before long, she was a good speaker. She told people about Franklin's ideas. She wrote articles for newspapers. She led political groups. She fought for laws that would help poor people.

Eleanor made speeches and told people about Franklin's ideas.

Political Partner

Franklin was able to return to politics with Eleanor's help. He ran for governor of New York and won in 1928.

Franklin still could not go everywhere he wanted. Eleanor went in his place. Eleanor visited schools, farms, and hospitals. She saw buildings that needed to be fixed. She talked to people who were hungry. After these visits, she told Franklin what she had seen. He worked to make things better. Eleanor also helped other women working in politics.

Franklin wanted to be president of the United States. Eleanor helped him run for office. Franklin became president in 1932. As his wife, Eleanor was now the First Lady of the United States.

Eleanor visited schools to talk with children.

First Lady

Many people in the United States had a hard time between 1929 and 1939. This was called the Great Depression. Thousands of people lost their jobs. Families went hungry.

Franklin was president from 1933 to 1945. He started a government program called the New Deal. The program created jobs and helped feed the hungry. Eleanor acted as her husband's eyes and ears. She traveled to big cities and small towns. She visited farms and coal mines. Eleanor told Franklin about what she saw and heard.

Eleanor wrote a newspaper column called "My Day." She also had a radio program. She told people what she and the president were doing to help.

People wrote to Eleanor when they had problems. Sometimes she received more than 30,000 letters a month. If she could not help, she tried to find someone who could.

Franklin was president from 1933 to 1945.

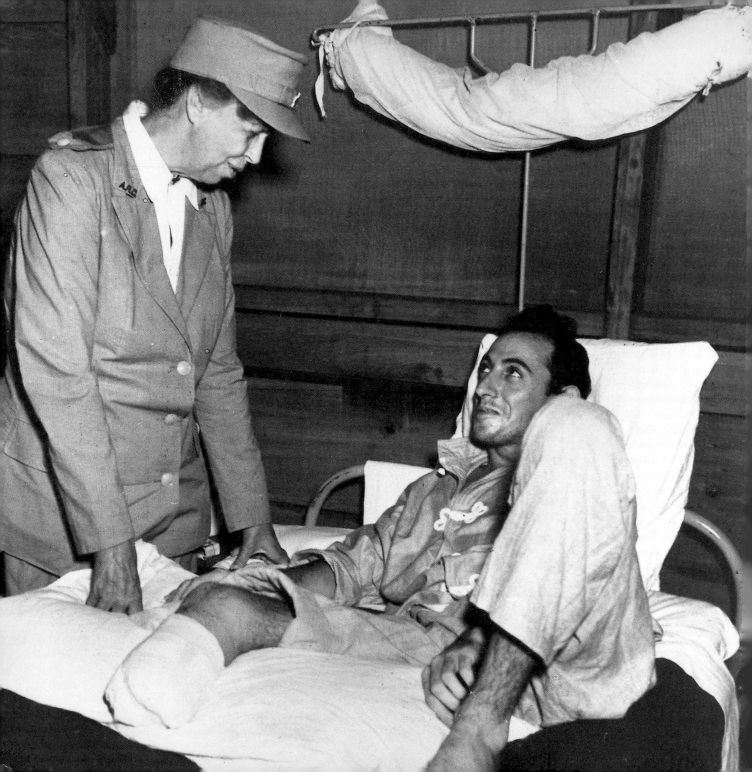

Working for Peace

Eleanor went back to her volunteer work after World War II (1939–1945) began. She traveled to army hospitals all over the world. Wounded U.S. soldiers enjoyed her visits. She raised their spirits. Eleanor also spoke out for women, African Americans, and all people in need.

Franklin was elected President four times. He worked hard to end World War II. Sadly, he died just before it ended in 1945.

Eleanor was no longer the First Lady. But she did not stop helping people. She wanted to put an end to war. In 1945, President Harry Truman asked her to join the U.S. delegation to the United Nations. There, Eleanor helped countries find ways to get along. She worked for peace and human rights.

Eleanor traveled to army hospitals all over the world.

First Lady of the World

Eleanor led an important group at the United Nations. This group wrote a paper. The paper was called the United Nations Universal Declaration of Human Rights. It said that all people are equal and should be treated fairly.

Eleanor traveled to many countries. She spread the United Nations' message of peace. President Truman called Eleanor the First Lady of the World.

Eleanor wrote books about her life and her ideas. She died on November 7, 1962, in New York City. People all over the world were sad. Millions of people felt they had lost a great leader.

The FDR Memorial opened on May 2, 1997, in Washington, D.C. A memorial is a monument. It is built to remember a person or happening. The FDR Memorial tells about Franklin Roosevelt. One of the rooms has a statue of Eleanor. This is the first statue to honor a First Lady in any presidential memorial.

Eleanor led an important group at the United Nations.

Words from Eleanor Roosevelt

"No one can make you feel inferior without your consent."

From a book by Eleanor Roosevelt, *You Learn by Living*, 1960.

"You gain strength, courage, and confidence by every experience in which you really stop to look fear in the face. . . . You must do the thing you think you cannot do."

From a book by Eleanor Roosevelt, *You Learn by Living*, 1960.

"Life was meant to be lived, and curiosity must be kept alive. One must never, for whatever reason, turn one's back on life."

From a book by Eleanor Roosevelt, *The Autobiography of Eleanor Roosevelt*, 1960.

Important Dates in Eleanor Roosevelt's Life

1884—Born on October 11 in New York City

1892—Mother Anna dies

1894—Father Elliott dies

1905—Marries Franklin Delano Roosevelt

1917—Begins volunteer work with Red Cross

1921—Franklin has polio; Eleanor begins going to meetings in his place

1928—Franklin is elected governor of New York

1932—Becomes First Lady when Franklin is elected president

1945—Franklin dies

1945–1952—Serves as U.S. delegate to the United Nations

1962—Dies on November 7 in New York City

Words to Know

delegation (del-uh-GAY-shuhn)—a group that speaks for a country

Great Depression (GRAYT di-PRESH-uhn)—period of hard times from 1929 to 1939 when many people in the United States lost their jobs

human rights (HYOO-muhn RITES)—the rights of all people to be treated fairly

polio (POH-lee-oh)—a disease that attacks the brain and spine

Red Cross (RED CROSS)—a worldwide group that helps people who are hurt by floods, wars, and other troubles

United Nations (yoo-NIE-tehd NAY-shunz)—a group of countries that works for peace

Read More

Faber, Doris. *Eleanor Roosevelt: First Lady to the World*. New York: Viking, 1985.

Jacobs, William Jay. *Eleanor Roosevelt: A Life of Happiness and Tears*. New York: Coward-McCann, 1983.

Weidt, Maryann N. *Stateswoman to the World: A Story about Eleanor Roosevelt*. Minneapolis: Carolrhoda Books, 1991.

Useful Addresses and Internet Sites

Eleanor Roosevelt
  National Historic Site
519 Albany Post Road
Hyde Park, NY 12538

Franklin D. Roosevelt Library
511 Albany Post Road
Hyde Park, NY 12538

Eleanor Roosevelt
http://www.msnbc.com/onair/msnbc/TimeAndAgain/archive/eleanor/default.asp

Eleanor Roosevelt: Always the First Lady
http://www.times.com/specials/magazine4/articles/roosevelt.html

FDR Memorial
http://www.axionet.com/key/FDR/Comm.html

Index